MCR

Spanish
r371.9092
Mach, J

Bilingual Titles from Finding My Way Books

Finding My Way Series

I Want To Be Like Poppin' Joe/Yo quiero ser como Joe Palomitas
Kaitlyn Wants To See Ducks/Kaitlyn quiere ver patos
I Don't Know If I Want a Puppy/Yo no sé si quiero un perrito
Marco and I Want To Play Ball/Marco y yo queremos jugar al béisbol
OE Wants It To Be Friday/OE quiere que sea viernes
Waylon Wants To Jam/Waylen quiere improvisar

Growing With Grace Series

MyaGrace Wants To Make Music/MyaGrace quiere hacer música
MyaGrace Wants To Get Ready/MyaGrace quiere alistarse

Learning My Way Series

Colors On My Papers/Rangi Za Makaratasi Yetu
Looking For Our Families/Kuangalia Familia Zetu
Fronts For Our Backs/Nyuso Kwa Migongo Yetu

For more titles visit www.findingmywaybooks.com

Waylen Wants To Jam

A True Story Promoting Inclusion and Self-Determination

Finding My Way Series

Waylen quiere improvisar

Una historia real que promueve la inclusión y la autodeterminación

Serie Encontrando mi camino

By/De Jo Meserve Mach
Vera Lynne Stroup-Rentier

Photography by/Fotografías de Mary Birdsell

Translation by/Traducción de
Karen Anchante

EVANSTON PUBLIC LIBRARY
1703 ORRINGTON AVENUE
EVANSTON, ILLINOIS 60201

TOPEKA, KANSAS

Library of Congress Control Number: 2016921224

Paperback ISBN: 978-1-9447645-2-4
Hardcover ISBN: 978-1-9447645-3-1

Text and photographs copyright © 2017 Finding My Way Books

Photographs by Mary Birdsell
Book design by Mary Birdsell

Educational Consultant Marla Conn

Spanish Translation by Karen Anchante

Finding My Way Books
honoring children with special needs or
disabilities by sharing their stories
www.findingmywaybooks.com

Finding My Way Books is dedicated to celebrating the success of inclusion by sharing stories about children with special needs in families and communities.

Finding My Way Books se dedica a celebrar el éxito de la inclusión al compartir historias acerca de niños con necesidades especiales en las familias y las comunidades.

We celebrate Waylen's story!

Waylen has autism. He is constantly challenged in how to communicate and participate, but he loves to drum. He always tells his mom, "I want to go drumming." Waylen is fortunate to have an incredibly supportive mother and extended family which allows him to participate in a community program. Because of Waylen's strong interest and this support, he succeeds on the drumline.

This success has started to change his life. Drumming is an extracurricular activity that could link to many opportunities as he ages. He feels like he belongs when he is drumming. Someday he will be playing in his school band and may become a member of a world famous rhythm and blues band.

We are so happy to share the hope revealed in this story!
~Jo, Vera and Mary

Por qué festejamos la historia de Waylen

Waylen tiene autismo. Para él, comunicarse y participar de actividades cotidianas es un desafio constante, pero a él le encanta tocar el tambor. Siempre le dice a su mamá: "Quiero ir a tocar el tambor". Waylen tiene la suerte de tener una madre y una familia increíblemente solidaria, lo que le permite participar en un programa comunitario. Debido al gran interés de Waylen y al apoyo que recibe, él tiene éxito en la banda de percursionistas.

Este éxito ha comenzado a cambiar su vida. Tocar el tambor es una actividad extracurricular que podría conducir a muchas otras oportunidades a medida que vaya creciendo. Él siente que pertenece al grupo cuando está tocando el tambor. Algún día él tocará el tambor en la banda de la escuela y quizás se convertirá en miembro de una banda de blues de fama mundial.

Nos sentimos muy contentas de compartir la esperanza que se revela en esta historia.
~Jo, Vera and Mary

Hi, my name is Waylen. I love to play the drums.
I play on a drumline.

Me llamo Waylen. Me encanta tocar el tambor.
Toco en una banda de percursionistas.

If you ask me how I play, I'll tell you, 1-2-3-4-5-6-7-8.
I count every time I hit the drum.

Si me preguntas como toco, te diré, 1-2-3-4-5-6-7-8.
Cuento cada vez que golpeo el tambor.

This is my drum class. I walk straight to my drum. I like being here!

Esta es mi clase de percusión. Voy directo al tambor. ¡Me gusta estar aquí!

Sal is our teacher. He tells us what to do.
He shows us what to do.

Sal es nuestro profesor. Él nos dice qué hacer.
Él nos muestra qué hacer.

Sal tells us how to "hold in" our sticks. That means we hold our sticks together. Then he shows us. I can hold in my sticks.

Sal nos muestra cómo "sostener" las baquetas. Eso significa que las mantengamos pegadas al cuerpo. Luego nos muestra cómo hacerlo. Yo puedo sostener mis baquetas.

Sal tells us how to hold our sticks to play. Then he shows us. He holds them in the fold of his fingers. I can hold my sticks like Sal.

Sal nos dice cómo agarrar nuestras baquetas para tocar. Luego nos muestra cómo hacerlo. Él las sostiene entre el pliegue de sus dedos. Yo puedo sostener mis baquetas como Sal.

Sal tells us how to place our sticks. Then he shows us. It looks like a slice of pizza. I can place my sticks like Sal.

Sal nos dice cómo colocar nuestras baquetas. Luego nos muestra. Parece una porción de pizza. Yo puedo colocar mis baquetas como Sal.

Sal tells us he's going to do a stick trick. Then he shows us. He throws his stick up and catches it. Wow! I want to try.

Sal nos dice que va a hacer un truco con una baqueta. Luego nos lo muestra. Él tira la baqueta en el aire y luego la atrapa. ¡Guau! Quiero intentarlo.

I try the stick trick. Whoops! My stick flew out of my hand. Whew! I'm glad it didn't hit anyone!

Intento hacer el truco de la baqueta. ¡Oh-oh! Mi baqueta se me escapó de la mano y salió volando. ¡Qué suerte! ¡Felizmente no le hice daño a nadie!

Sal says it's time to learn a song. We need to hold in our sticks and watch Sal. It's hard to wait and not play.

Sal dice que es hora de aprender una canción.
Necesitamos sostener nuestras baquetas y observar a Sal.
Es difícil esperar y no tocar.

Sal tells us the song is 'Hit-The-Drum.'
He says the beat matches the words.

Sal nos dice que la canción se llama "Toca el tambor".
Él dice que el tiempo coincide con las palabras.

He shows us how to 'Hit-The-Drum.' He hits the drum with his right hand. He hits the drum with his left hand. He hits the drum with his right hand, again.

Él nos muestra cómo tocar "Toca el tambor". Él toca el tambor con la mano derecha. Él toca el tambor con la mano izquierda. Él toca el tambor con la mano derecha otra vez.

Now we play with Sal. I hit the drum with my right hand. I hit the drum with my left hand. I hit the drum with my right hand, again.

Ahora tocamos con Sal. Yo toco el tambor con la mano derecha. Yo toco el tambor con la mano izquierda. Yo toco el tambor con la mano derecha otra vez.

Oops! I hit the drum next to me. It's hard to stop.
I love to play the drums!

Oh-oh, toqué el tambor que estaba al lado mío.
Es difícil parar.
Me encanta tocar el tambor.

Sal starts jamming. He plays a fun beat.
He wants us to copy his beat.

Sal empieza a improvisar. Él toca un ritmo divertido.
Él quiere que sigamos su tiempo.

We listen to Sal and play our drums. Sometimes I close my eyes. That makes it easier to hear Sal.

Escuchamos a Sal y tocamos nuestros tambores.
A veces cierro los ojos.
Eso hace más fácil escuchar a Sal.

This is so fun.
I can't stop playing.

Esto es tan divertido.
No puedo dejar de tocar.

Sal calls my name. He looks into my eyes. He tells me it's time to stop. I can see he cares. I stop playing.

Sal me llama. Me mira a los ojos. Me dice que es momento de parar. Me doy cuenta que le importa. Yo dejo de tocar.

Sal says if we don't play together, we just make noise.
We want to make music.

Sal dice que si no tocamos juntos, sólo hacemos ruido.
Y lo que queremos es hacer música.

Sal says to hold in our sticks. We aren't paying attention.
We need to listen better.

Sal dice que sostengamos nuestras baquetas.
No estamos prestando atención.
Necesitamos escuchar cuidadosamente.

We try again. Sal starts jamming.
Now, we pay attention.

Lo intentamos de nuevo. Sal empieza a improvisar.
Ahora sí prestamos atención.

Everyone is listening. We're learning to play like Sal. On a drumline, everyone must play the same way.

Todos están escuchando. Estamos aprendiendo a tocar como Sal. En una banda de percursionistas, todos deben tocar de la misma manera.

Sal wants us to take turns playing the bass drum.
Waiting in line is hard. I like to sit. I can keep the beat.

Sal quiere que nos turnemos para tocar el bombo.
Esperar en fila es difícil. Me gusta sentarme.
Puedo mantener el tiempo.

I can practice my stick trick.
This helps me wait.

Puedo practicar el truco de la baqueta.
Esto me ayuda a esperar.

It's my turn! I get some help.
The teen helpers are great drummers.

¡Es mi turno! Recibo ayuda.
Los asistentes jóvenes son grandes percursionistas.

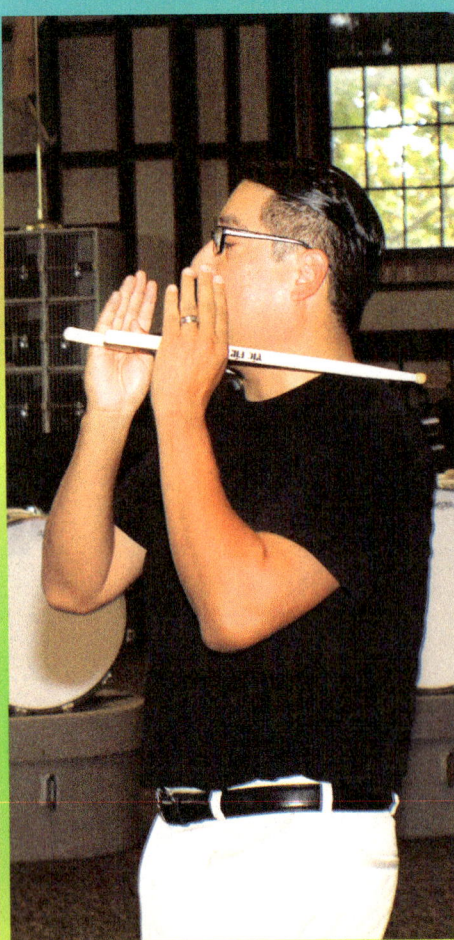

I'm back playing the snare drum. Sal shows us a drumline move. He steps and hits the drum. He yells, "I-I-I." Then he makes a silly pose on the beat.

Vuelvo a tocar la tarola. Sal nos muestra cómo movernos en línea. Él da un paso al frente y toca el tambor. Él grita, "I-I-I" Luego hace un gesto tonto al tiempo de la música.

Now I'll try. I step and hit.
"I-I-I." I'm silly like Sal.

Ahora lo intentamos todos. Yo doy un paso al frente y toco.
"I-I-I" Soy gracioso como Sal.

We all try again, before practice ends. We're learning to do everything together. We have to get ready for our concert.

Lo intentamos todos de nuevo, antes de que termine la práctica. Estamos aprendiendo a hacer todo juntos. Tenemos que alistarnos para nuestro concierto.

The time has come! Our concert is starting.
We are lined up and ready to play.

¡Ha llegado la hora! Ya empieza nuestro concierto.
Estamos alineados y listos para tocar.

We play the songs we learned. We do the moves we practiced.
I try my best.

Tocamos las canciones que aprendimos.
Hacemos los movimientos que practicamos.
Hago lo mejor que puedo.

We bow on the last beat. Our concert is finished.
This is our drumline.

Hacemos una reverencia en el último tiempo.
Nuestro concierto ha terminado.
Esta es nuestra banda de percursionistas.

I love playing the drums.
I know this is where I belong.

Me encanta tocar el tambor.
Sé que aquí es donde debo estar.

Thank you to Waylen and Sal for sharing their story.

Gracias a Waylen y a Sal por compartir su historia.

Vocabulary Glossary
Glosario de Vocabulario

Hold in - bring sticks together close to your body
Sostener - Mantener las baquetas juntas pegadas al cuerpo

Snare drum - small drum
Tarola - Tambor pequeño

Bass drum - big drum
Bombo - Tambor grande

Jamming - making music with feeling
Improvisar - Hacer música con sentimiento

Silly pose - standing so you look funny
Postura tonta - Pararse de manera graciosa

Drumline move - action everyone on the drumline does together
Desplazamiento de la banda de percusionistas - Acción que todos los integrantes de la banda de percusionistas tienen que ejecutar juntos.

36

Encouraging self-determination skill building in children

Our books are written in the actual voice of a child. The child is telling their story of how they are learning to be more self-determined.

Here are examples of self-determination skills:
1. Choice making
2. Decision making
3. Problem solving
4. Goal setting and planning
5. Self-direction behaviors (self-regulation)
6. Responsibility
7. Independence
8. Self-awareness and self-knowledge
9. Self-advocacy and leadership
10. Communication
11. Participation
12. Having relationships and social connections

Weir, K., Cooney, M., Walter, M., Moss, C., & Carter, E. W. (2011). Fostering self-determination among children with disabilities: Ideas from parents for parents. *Madison, WI: Natural Supports Project, Waisman Center, University of Wisconsin—Madison.*

Discussion Starters and Activities To Promote Self-Determination

Providing Participation:
Story pages demonstrating participation: 3, 7, 10, 11, 14, 16, 19, 20, 22, 23, 25, 28-31

Discussion starter:
Because communication is such a challenge for Waylen he has to work very hard to focus and participate. Sometimes it feels overwhelming and it seems the only thing to do is to lie down and rest, but Waylen loves to drum. He loves the feel of his sticks hitting the drum! His interest motivates him to try as hard as he can to fully participate. What is an activity you participate in that you love? When is it hard for you to participate? Why?

Classroom activity:
Distribute pictures of instruments to students. Have the students find their group based on the type of insturments. (Strings, brass, woodwinds, percussion) Each group will work together to prepare a pantomime to show the class how the instruments in their section are played.

Ask students to share what they liked about participating in this activity and what they didn't like.

For Self Direction:
Story pages demonstrating self-direction: 5, 7, 13, 16, 23, 24, 27, 30

Discussion starter:
It's a challenge following directions in a large room with 25 students and 25 loud drums. Sal gives directions by telling students what to do and then showing them how to do it. Can you remember Sal's directions for an activity? (For example: Sal says to hold your sticks like a piece of pizza. Then he holds up his sticks in the air and shows what a piece of pizza looks like.)

Sometimes, there is waiting time while everyone takes a turn doing an activity. How does Waylen keep himself waiting quietly? What do you remember about the picture of him hitting the floor with his sticks so he can keep the rhythm he likes? He self directs so he can feel in control. What do you do to keep yourself in control? How do you self direct?

Classroom activity:
Divide the class into two groups. One group of students can talk loudly to each other for three minutes. Ask the other students to do an activity of their own choosing (self-directing) to help them feel in control during the time of chaos. After three minutes ask the students that completed self-directed activities to share their feelings about their choice of activity and how successful they were in staying in control. Repeat this activity while switching roles of the two groups.

For Communication and Social Connections:
Story pages demonstrating communication and social connections: 1, 2, 9, 17, 18, 23, 25, 28, 30

Discussion starter:
Sal is a very good communicator. He tells the students what to do and then he shows them how to do it. Sal is very animated and consistent in sharing his expectations. He uses his voice, his actions, and his expression to communicate. Waylen and the other students understand what Sal is asking them to do.

It is difficult for Waylen to share what he needs or wants, because Waylen has autism. Sometimes his facial expressions don't match his feelings; both speaking and showing what he feels is a challenge. When have you had difficulty sharing how you were feeling?

Classroom activity:
Provide students with two pencils or sticks. Have students sit in pairs facing each other with a desk between them. Students are to take turns teaching their partner a simple rhythm with their sticks. Each student needs to tell his/her partner what to do and then show his/her partner how to do it.

Ask students to draw a picture of how they look when they are drumming. They need to show expressions on their faces. How does drumming make them feel? Ask students to share their pictures and their feelings.

For Choice Making
Story pages demonstrating choice making: 3, 5, 9, 14, 21, 27, 32

Discussion starter:
When he was youger, Waylen always liked banging on things and he enjoyed watching his older brother play the drums. Waylen wants to be a drummer, too. What do you like to do? How do your interests help you make choices?

Classroom activity:
Ask students to share their interests by writing about them or drawing a picture of them. Taking turns, ask students to describe their interests to their classmates. Make a large graph showing common interests. Then group interests into categories and create a new graph showing the categories.

Free downloadable lessons are available at: www.findingmywaybooks.com

Additional resources linked to Finding My Way Books titles
are available at: www.teacherspayteachers.com

42

Jo Meserve Mach, author and publisher, spent 36 years as an Occupational Therapist. She is very passionate about sharing the stories of children with special needs. Jo embraces the joy that individuals with disabilities bring to our communities through their unique gifts.

Vera Lynne Stroup-Rentier, author, worked as a professional in Early Childhood Education and Special Education programming for 25 years. She has a PhD in Special Education from the University of Kansas and is currently working at the Kansas State Department of Education. Vera is passionate about the inclusion of each and every child in settings where they would be if they did not have a disability. Parenting a teen and tween with special needs enrich her life.

Mary Birdsell is a professional photographer and a former Speech and Theatre teacher. She strives to create images that reflect the strengths of each child. Mary's background in education, theatre and photography intersect as she visually creates our books. She uses colors and shapes to tell a story. For her, each book is like it's own theatrical production.

Karen Anchante, translator, has over 20 years of experience teaching languages. She has a Ph.D. in Spanish from Arizona State University. As a mother of two young children, she loves contributing to enriching projects that benefit children. She is also a fervent believer of the effective power of reading from an early age.

Cruzline is a percussion drumline directed by Sal Cruz.

For more information visit:
www.cruzlinepercussion.com

For more information:
www.findingmywaybooks.com

Contact us:
info@findingmywaybooks.com

CPSIA information can be obtained
at www.ICGtesting.com
Printed in the USA
FSOW03n2351240417
33366FS